THE ART OF ALUMINUM FOIL

The Art of Aluminum Foil

JANE HINTON and HUGH OLIVER

GENERAL PUBLISHING COMPANY LIMITED   *Don Mills, Ontario*

First published 1974 by General Publishing Limited

ISBN 0-7736-1014-6

Design/Peter Maher & Associates

Printed and bound in Canada

1 2 3 4 5 AP 78 77 76 75 74

In the making of this book, Jane Hinton
was responsible for the foil creations and
Hugh Oliver for writing the text. Both
of them gratefully acknowledge the
contribution of David Stevenson,
Manager of Packaged Foils for Alcan
Canada Products Limited, who not only
conceived the idea of the book but was
also very helpful in bringing it to fruition.

Contents

Introduction — Starting with Foil

Of the many new materials that offer a challenge to the artistic imagination, one of the most appealing is aluminum foil. It is inexpensive and readily available. Its bright metallic surface is visually attractive and eye-catching, and it is simple to work with. As we show in the following pages, a roll of household foil opens up a host of creative possibilities, ranging from simple decorations that a small child can make to reliefs for permanent display.

It is not essential to know what foil is in order to make things with it, any more than it is necessary to understand the nature of pigments in order to paint a picture. At the same time, knowledge of the material you are using may help to provide some insight into its scope and limitations.

Manufacture of Aluminum Foil—To manufacture foil, slabs of aluminum metal (known as ingot) are passed to and fro between rollers to reduce their thickness. The foil that emerges from the final set of rollers is less than 0.006 inch thick.

In the final rolling operation, two sheets of foil backing onto each other pass through the rollers at the same time. The foil surfaces exposed to the rollers emerge very shiny; the surfaces backing onto each other are much duller. When making

things with foil, it is usually desirable to have the shiny surface showing.

Properties of Aluminum Foil—Aluminum foil has the properties of its parent metal, aluminum. Some of the more important of these properties are as follows:
- —light weight (for the same volume, it is about a third as heavy as iron or copper)
- —resists corrosion
- —easy to fabricate (which is essential in the rolling operation for manufacturing foil)
- —good electrical conductor
- —excellent reflector (which is an important attribute of the foil decorations described in this book)

Types of Aluminum Foil and Their Uses
- —household regular: cooking, packaging, etc.
- —household heavy-duty: packaging
- —gift wrap: festive packaging
- —florist: for wrapping potted plants
- —hobby: a more expensive and heavier foil that requires very precise cutting and folding – generally beyond the scope of this book.

Rolling Aluminum Foil

Some General Points

1. In the materials list preceding the instructions for projects in this book, we have noted all the materials you need to make each item. But there are some materials that you will continually need – Scotch tape, rubber cement, scissors, thread, and a 12-inch ruler.

2. Household regular foil is the most suitable kind of foil to make the majority of decorations described in this book. But for a few things the greater strength of household heavy-duty foil is desirable. The kind of foil is specified at the end of each materials list.

3. Although you can tear off the foil using the serrated edge on the box top, you will get a neater edge if you tear the foil against a ruler (see fig. 1, page 4).

4. As explained in the introduction, one side of a piece of foil has a shiny finish and the other side a mat finish. In all the things that you make, the shiny side of the foil should form the surface that shows. Where this is not obvious, we have made a note in the instructions.

5. We have tried to be as explicit as possible in our instructions, and we hope that the combination of photographs and text has eliminated ambiguities as far as is possible in a book of this kind. But we should point out that the "art of aluminum foil" doesn't have to be a very precise one. Although in most instances we have specified dimensions and techniques with exactness, you can freely modify these to your own needs and specifications; and if you get into difficulties, you will find that foil is a very adaptable material – a patch here, a scissor cut there, another piece of masking tape, or a squeeze with your fingers will often put things right.

Some of the techniques for working with foil will now be discussed and a number of things you can make will be described. But once you have become familiar with the material, it is your own imagination that should guide you. You will find that there is plenty of scope and that you can go on to create a glittering display of beautiful things.

1 Decorations for Hanging

In this section, we describe how to make decorations that can be hung around a room, on a Christmas tree or, if you wish, outdoors. Several of them are simple enough for a small child to make, and none of them require any special skill. The decorations are particularly suitable for Christmas, but they will add glitter to any festive occasion.

To make Christmas Bells

Materials:
— Four paper cups or plastic yogurt containers
— Four small bells (available from gift wrap section of department stores) or small silver baubles (available where Christmas tree decorations are sold)
— Scotch tape
— Tinsel cord
— Scissors
— Velvet ribbon
— Sprig of holly (real or plastic)
— Regular foil

Instructions:
1. Tear off a 12-inch piece of foil. Starting at one corner, wrap it around one of the cups. Flatten over the base,

smooth round the sides, and smooth overlap neatly around the inside of the cup (figs. 1,2). Secure with Scotch tape where necessary. Repeat with remaining cups.

2. Tie a 10-inch length of tinsel cord to one of the bells or baubles. Make a hole with scissor points through the top of one of the inverted cups (fig. 3). Then, making a knot in the cord so the bell hangs just below the rim of the cup, thread the cord up through

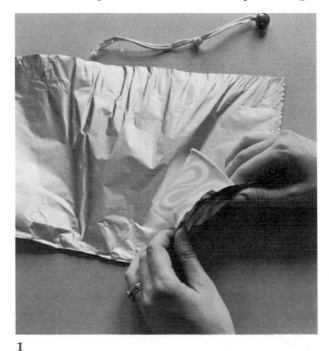

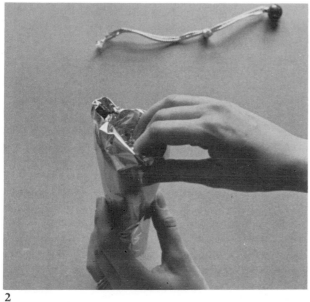

2

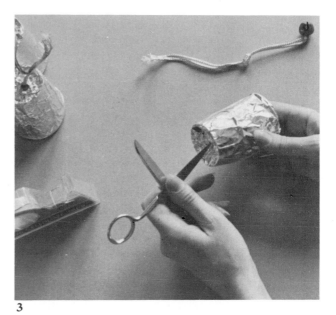

3

4

5

the hole in the cup (fig. 4). Repeat with the remaining cups, and knot all the cups together with the four lengths of emerging cord (fig. 5).

3. Attach a bow of velvet ribbon and a sprig of holly to the knot where the four bells are gathered.

To make Decorative Chains

There are several different kinds of chains that you can make with foil. Here are four of them.

A Chain of Rings

Materials:

—Regular foil

Instructions:

1. Tear the foil into pieces that are approximately 12 inches square (fig. 1). (*Note:* With smaller squares of foil, you can make a chain with smaller rings.)
2. Roll one of the squares into a "snake", using your index finger to keep the "mouth" of the snake open (figs. 2,3).
3. Loop into a circle by inserting the tail of the snake into its open mouth, and mould with your fingers to form a solid ring (fig. 4).
4. Repeat with the next square, threading the snake through the first ring before inserting its tail in its mouth (fig. 5).
5. Repeat with more squares for as long as you wish to make the chain.

1

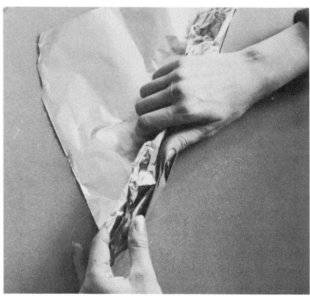

2

3

4

5

6

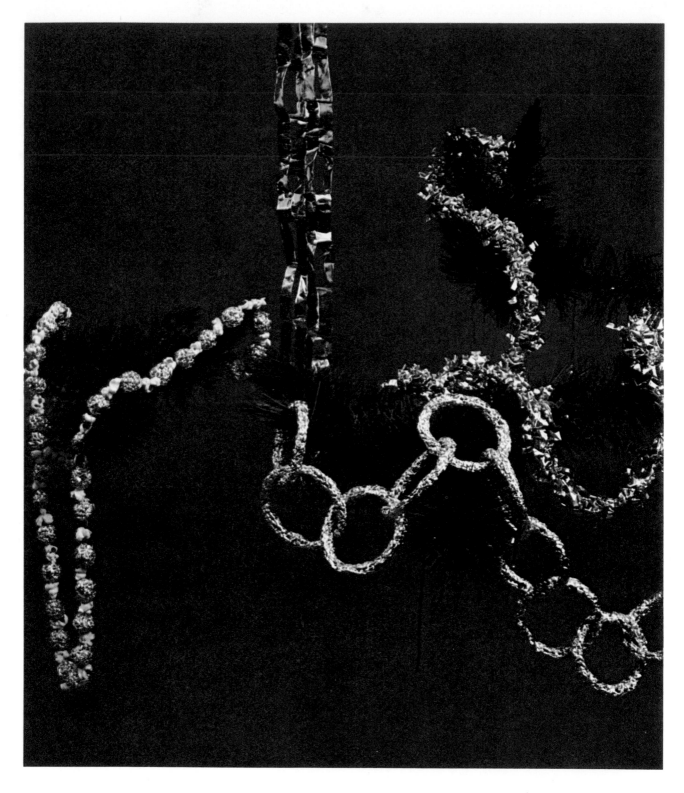

Popcorn Chain

Materials:
  —Popcorn
  —Needle and heavy thread
  —Regular foil

Instructions:
  1. Crumple up foil scraps into small balls about 1 inch in diameter – foil leftovers from other things you may have been making are handy here.
  2. Knot one end of the thread, and with the needle, thread on first a foil ball, then a piece of popcorn, then a foil ball, alternately for as long as you wish to make the chain.

Note: Small children find this chain easy and enjoyable to make.

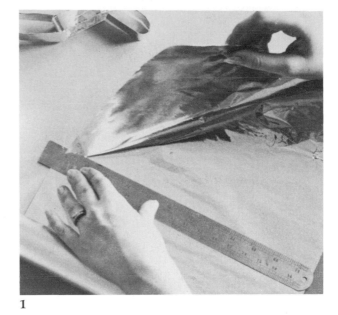

1

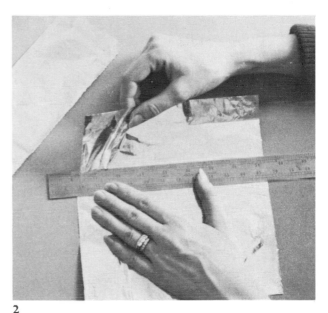

2

Looped Chain

Materials:
  —Scotch tape
  —Regular foil

Instructions:
  1. Tear off an 8-inch strip of foil, and then tear into four pieces 8 inches by 3 inches (figs. 1,2).

2. Fold in both edges of one piece lengthwise so that they meet at the centre, and flatten. Then fold in half so that the outer edges meet to form a band approximately ¾ inch wide. Flatten out the band so that it is firm (figs. 3,4,5). (*Note:* This technique for making a band of foil is referred to quite frequently in other instructions later in the book.)

3. Loop the two ends of the band together, and crimp the overlapping ends firmly a couple of times to join them. Alternatively, if you have problems, you can join the ends with

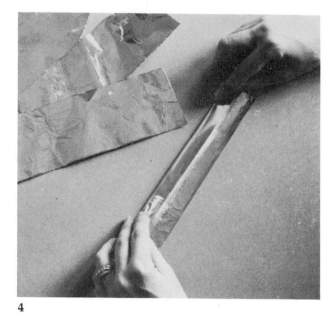

4

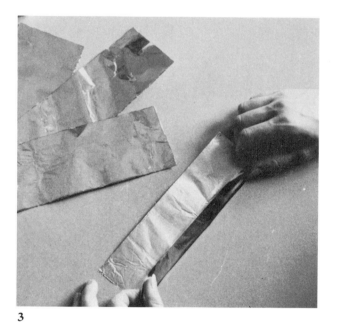

3

5

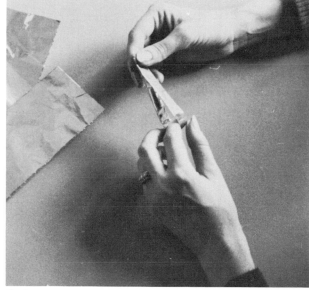

6

7

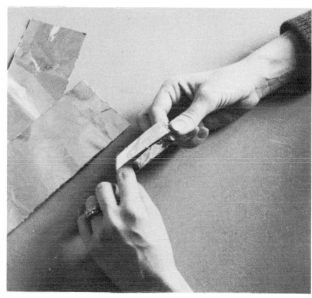

8

9

Scotch tape. Open up with your finger or a pencil to form a loop (figs. 6,7,8).

4. Repeat with the next piece of foil, looping the band through the first loop before joining the ends (fig. 9).
5. Repeat with more pieces for as long as you wish to make the chain.

Fringed Rope

Materials:
—String
—Scissors
—Regular foil

Instructions:
1. Tear off several 3½-inch strips of foil.
2. Fold a strip in half lengthwise, and working along the open edges, cut fringes at ¼-inch intervals to within about ¼ inch of the fold. Children's blunt scissors are generally the right length for making the cuts (fig. 1).
3. Wrap the uncut fold spirally around the string, pressing it firmly and ensuring that the string is covered. Splay out the fringes (fig. 2).
4. Repeat with another strip of foil, ensuring that you have overlap with the first strip; at the joint, you can mould the fringes from each strip together.
5. Repeat with more strips of foil until you have covered the string.

1

2

To make Decorative Stars

Again, there are several different kinds of stars that you can make with foil. Here are three of them.

An Asterisk Star

Materials:
—Drinking straws
—Tinsel cord
—Scissors
—Scotch tape
—Heavy thread
—Regular foil

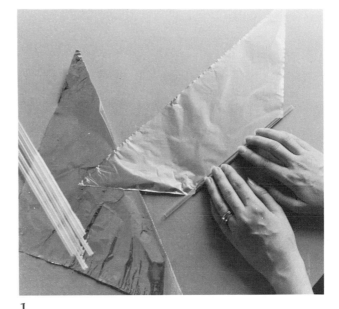

1

Instructions:
1. Tear off a 12-inch strip of foil to give a 12-inch square. Cut in half diagonally to form two triangles.
2. Place a drinking straw at the tip of one of the triangles (i.e., at the 90-degree angle), roll the foil around it, and secure with Scotch tape. Twist the foil overlap at each end of the straw and trim with scissors to a point (figs. 1,2).
3. In this way, make three (or four) foil-covered straws. Holding them together at their centres so that they spread out to form the points of a star, weave them securely with tinsel cord. Loop the cord up and over the straws a couple of times and knot at the back (fig. 3).
4. To hang the star, attach heavy thread through one of the foil tips. See photo, bottom of page 15.

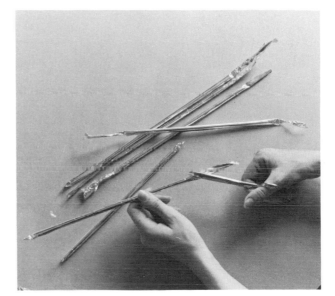

2

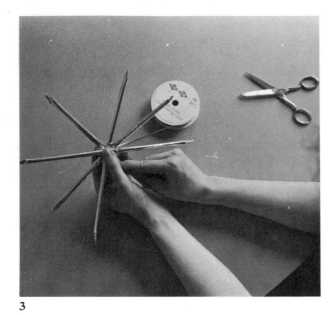

3

Note: It is possible with two foil-covered straws to make what is known as the "Eye-of-God" design. The two straws are centred at right angles to each other, and using two colours of tinsel cord, the weave is extended out from the centre (see drawing).

diagram of how to weave "The eye of God" Star

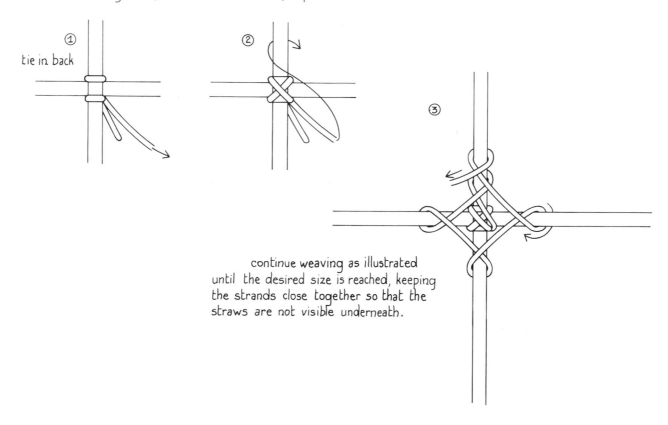

① tie in back

②

③

continue weaving as illustrated until the desired size is reached, keeping the strands close together so that the straws are not visible underneath.

A Satellite Star

Materials:
- —Small styrofoam ball, about 1 inch in diameter
- —Toothpicks
- —Scissors
- —Heavy thread
- —Regular foil

Instructions:
1. Wrap a piece of foil firmly round the styrofoam ball.
2. Roll a dozen or so toothpicks in small triangles of foil, flattening the foil at the larger end of each toothpick and trimming with scissors to a point. Insert the smaller ends of the toothpicks into the ball, and arrange them in a suitable design.
3. To hang the star, attach thread through one of the foil tips.

Note: This star is simple for small children to make. See bottom picture, page 15.

Snow Crystal Star

Materials:
- —Scotch tape
- —Heavy thread
- —Regular foil

Instructions:
1. To create the foil star in the photograph at the top of page 15, make six bands of foil 10 inches long and six bands of foil 6 inches long (see instructions 1 and 2 on pages 7-8).
2. Take one of the 10-inch bands and one of the 6-inch bands and, with the smaller band on the inside, loop all four ends together (fig. 1). Crimp the ends to hold them together, and open out to form a teardrop shape (fig. 2). Repeat with the other bands.

1

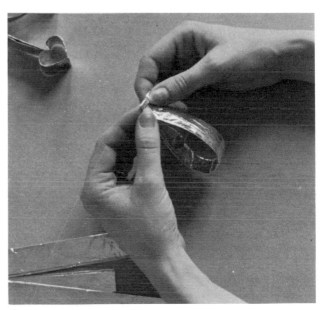

2

3

4

3. Make a band of foil 6 inches long and loop the ends together to form a circle, joining with Scotch tape. Around this circle, tape the six teardrop shapes (fig. 3).
4. Make six bands of foil 8 inches long. At one end of each band, shape the band into a heart and tape the end onto the band stem. Tape the other ends of these bands onto the central circle, interspersing them between the teardrops (fig. 4).

Note: Using this technique, it is possible to make a variety of different designs (see adjacent figs.). It requires a little patience but the results can be very attractive. When hanging the stars, it is often more convenient to attach a wire hook to the free end of the thread.

Snow Crystal

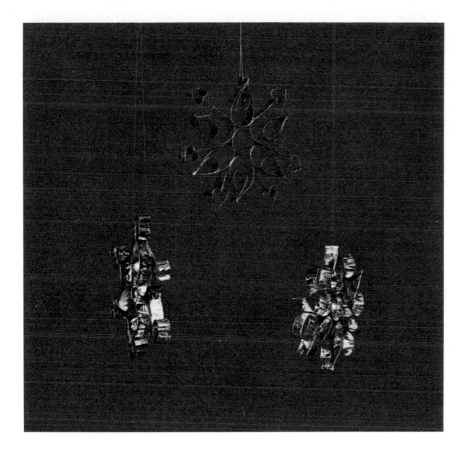

To make a Pom-Pom

1

Materials:
- —Scissors
- —Coloured string
- —Scotch tape
- —Rubber cement
- —Foil gift wrap or coloured paper
- —Regular foil

Instructions:

1. Cut out four circles of regular foil and four circles of gift wrap or coloured paper (fig. 1). How big you make the circles depends on how large you want the pom-pom to be. Anywhere between 3 inches and 12 inches is a good beginning.

2. Fold each circle in half, with the shiny or design surface facing inwards. Then place the half-circles on top of each other with the foil and gift wrap alternating in the pile (figs. 2, 3). Glue the adjacent half-circles together through the pile.

3. Tape coloured string along the straight edge of the top half-circle. Then open out and glue the top and bottom half-circles together to form a ball (fig. 4).

2

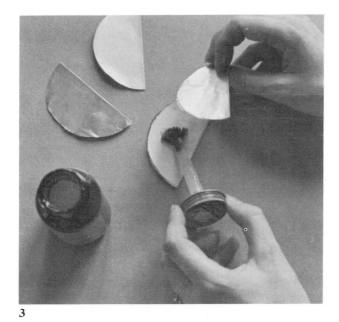

3

Note: This is another decoration that small children can easily make.

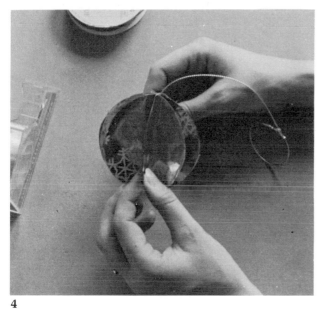

4

To make a Christmas Wreath

Materials:
—Styrofoam ring, about 9 inches in diameter (or larger, if you wish); these rings may be bought from a hobby shop
—Pins
—Hairpins
—Bent wire hook
—Satin ribbon
—Six small silver baubles (tree decorations)
—Regular or heavy-duty foil

Instructions:
1. Tear a sheet of foil into pieces that are approximately 3 inches square. Make rosettes by pinching each piece in the centre (to form the stem), and roughly moulding the edges to form a rose-like shape (figs. 2,3,4).
2. Pin each rosette through the stem onto the styrofoam ring, poking the pins firmly with the end of a pencil. Spacing the rosettes about 1 inch apart so that they overlap, cover the top and sides of the ring (figs. 5,6).

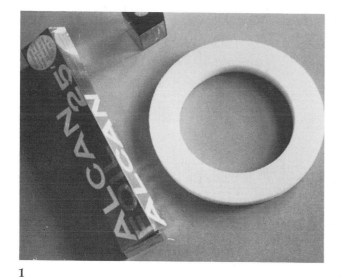

1

2

3

4

5

6

7

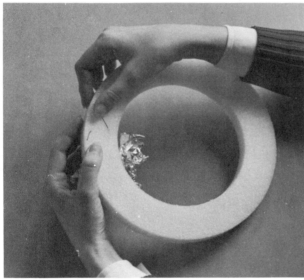

8

3. Loop the attachment on each silver bauble onto a hairpin. Space the baubles at intervals round the wreath, by pushing the ends of each hairpin through the styrofoam and bending the ends flat as they emerge at the back (figs. 7,8).
4. Loop the bent wire hook onto a hairpin. Push in the ends of the hairpin from the back of the wreath.
5. Make a bow out of two lengths of satin ribbon and, using a hairpin again, attach the bow to the base of the wreath.

To make a Model Bird

Materials:
—Styrofoam tray from meat market or sheet of cardboard
—Scotch tape
—Scissors
—Piece of gift wrap
—Rubber cement
—About 20 inches of tinsel cord
—Blunt knitting needle
—Regular foil

Instructions:
1. Draw a simple design on styrofoam sheet, using the diagram on page 21 to guide you. Cut out the design (figs. 1,2).
2. Tear off about 12 inches of foil and place the cut-out on top of the dull side.
3. Roughly cut the foil around the design, leaving about a 2-inch margin.
4. Cut the foil at about 1-inch intervals up to the edge of the design (fig. 3).

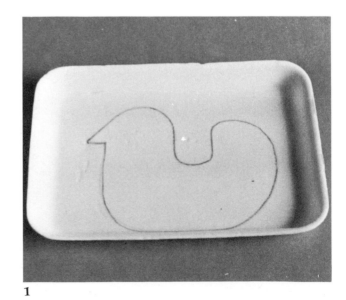

1

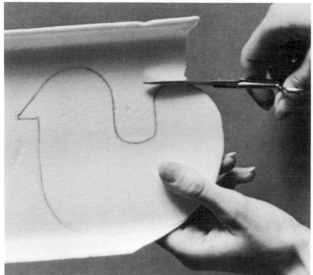

2

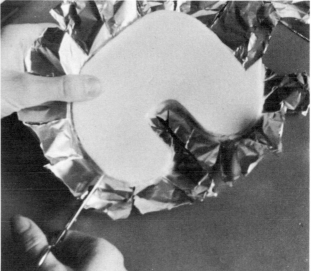

3

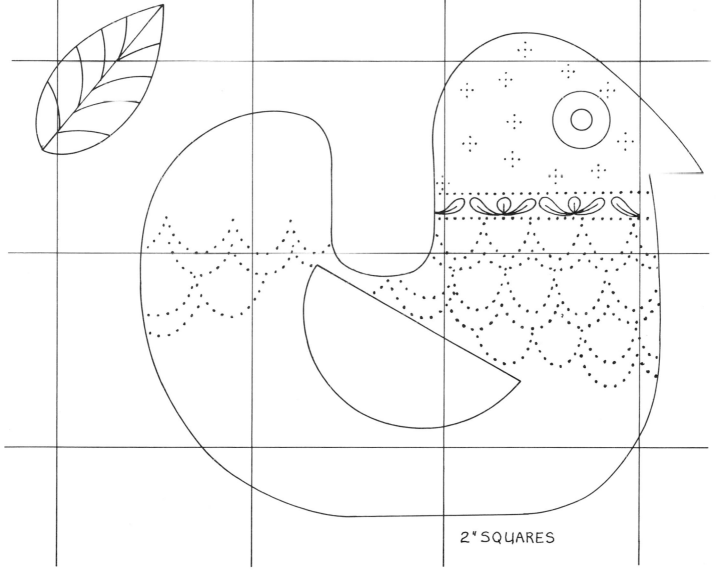

2" SQUARES

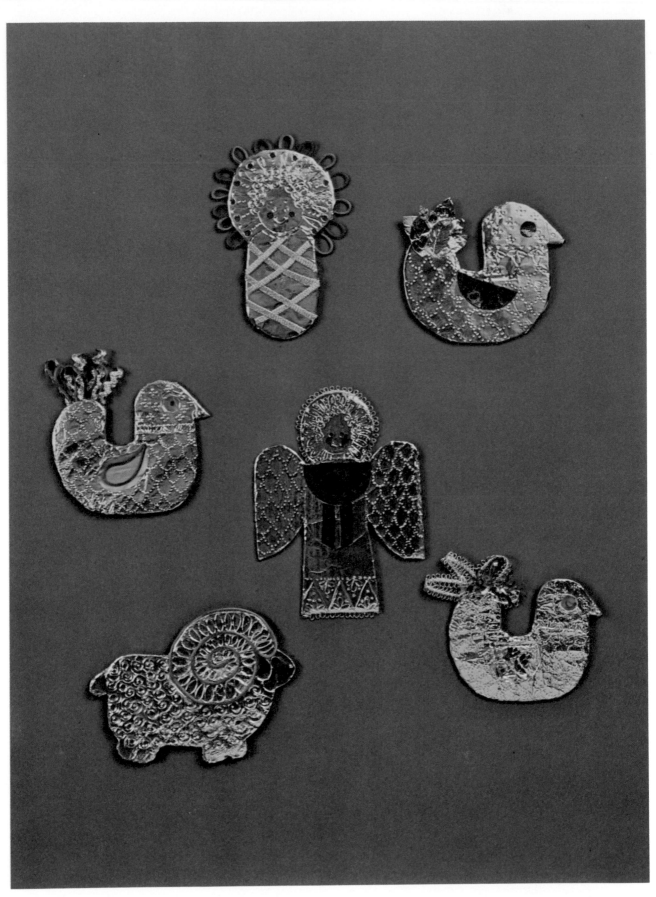

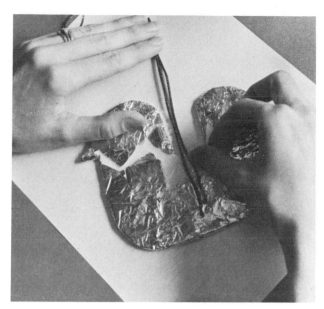

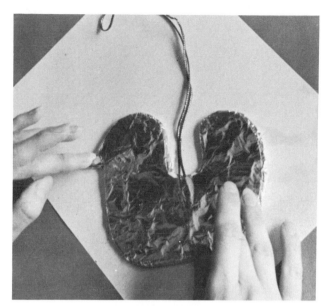

4

5

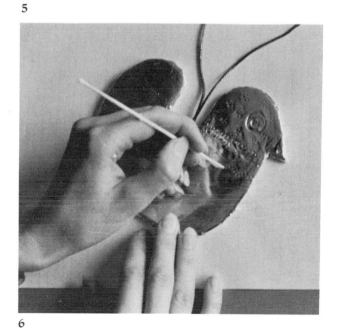

6

5. Fold the foil around the design, being careful not to tear it when folding over projections (for example, the beak).

6. Double the tinsel cord into a loop, and with Scotch tape fasten the ends to the back of the design, approximately in the centre (fig. 4).

7. Cut a second piece of foil to a shape about ¼ inch smaller than the original design. Shiny side up, glue on the back to cover ragged edges (fig. 5).

8. With a blunt knitting needle, engrave dots on the front surface of the design to form feather patterns (see diagram page 21 and fig. 6).

9. To make the eye and the wing, cut out the pieces of foil gift wrap and glue on the surface.

10. To make the tail, draw feather patterns with a blunt knitting needle on a piece of foil (the foil should be resting on a resilient surface such as cardboard). Cut out the feathers and glue them to the design to form the tail plumage. If you wish, sequins or buttons may be glued to the surface to enhance the design, or the tail can be made from lace trim.

design for angel

1 square = 1"

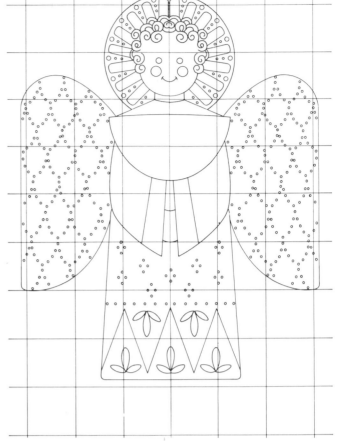

design for Ram

1 square = 1"

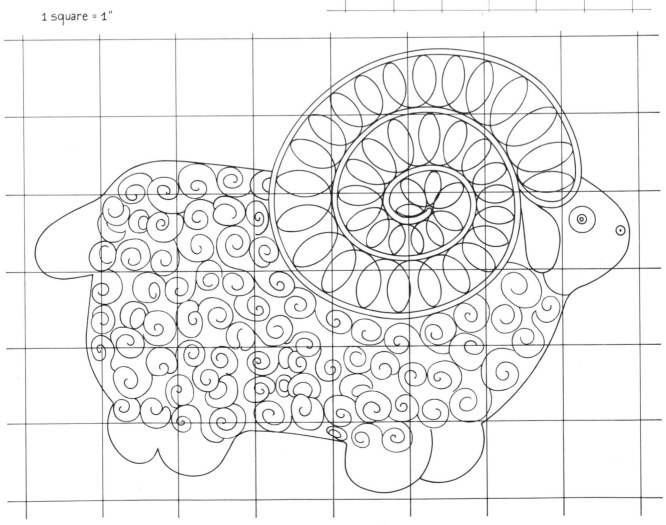

2 Table Decorations

The decorations described in this section are particularly suitable for decorating the table at Christmas time or for a child's birthday party. But they will of course enhance the look of the table on any special dining occasion.

To make a Christmas Tree

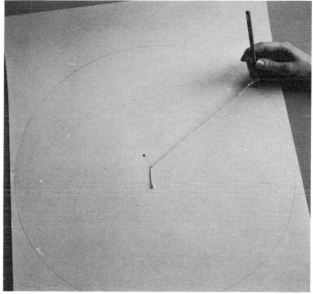

1

Materials:
- Sheet of heavy paper or light cardboard, about 20 inches square
- Masking tape or staples
- Scotch tape
- Scissors
- Hairpin
- Heavy-duty foil

Instructions:
1. Cut a circle with a radius of approximately 10 inches from the paper or cardboard. If you don't have a large pair of compasses, you can draw the circle by pinning a length of string firmly to the centre, measuring off 10 inches on the string, and looping the free end onto a pencil (fig. 1).

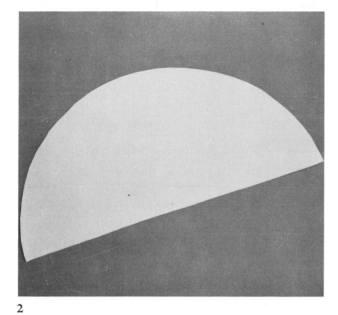

2

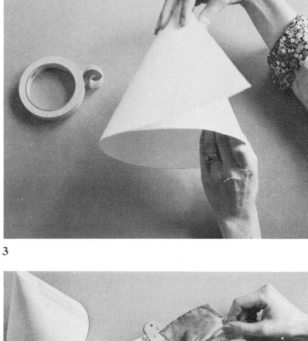

3

4

5

2. Cut the circle in half (fig. 2). You will need one half for the Christmas tree. Keep the other half – you can use it to make the Christmas Angel described later in this section (page 35).

3. Fold the half-circle into the shape of a cone by wrapping it round your hand. The diameter at the base of the cone should be approximately 5½ inches. Join the sides of the cone with masking tape or staples (figs. 3,4).

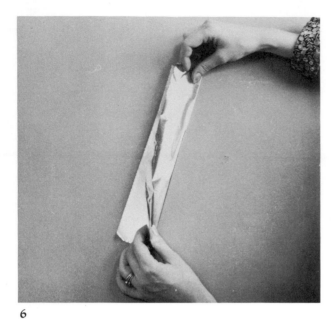

6

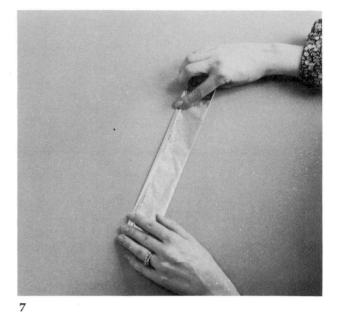

7

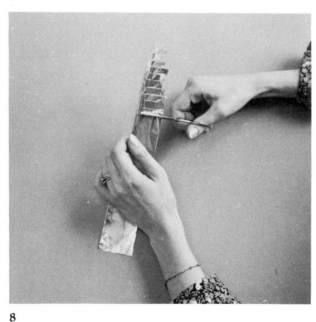

8

9

4. Tear off several 4-inch strips of foil. Fold each strip in half lengthwise to form a band 18 inches long and 2 inches wide. Then make a ¼-inch fold along the open edges to join them and form a reinforcement (figs. 5,6,7). Working along the edge of the first fold, cut fringes at about ¼-inch intervals up to the edge of the reinforcement (fig. 8).

5. With thumb and index finger, gently curve out the fringes (fig. 9). Then begin taping the reinforced edge to the cone, starting at the base and applying a piece of Scotch tape every 3 inches. The fringes should be pointing down from the reinforced edge and then curving out and up (fig. 10).

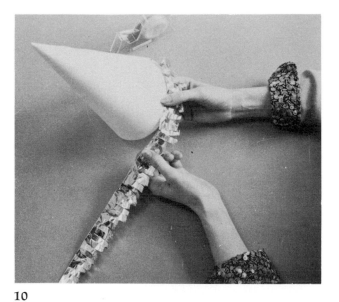

10

11

6. Proceed spirally up the cone, where necessary taking in small tucks along the reinforced edge to adjust to the cone's shape. The distance between the reinforced edge round each spiral should be about ½ inch, or enough so that the fringes overlap the cone surface beneath (fig. 11). Continue up the cone until it is completely covered (fig. 12).

7. With a hairpin and a piece of tape, attach a foil star or Christmas bauble to the top of the tree and place "gifts" (match or other small boxes wrapped in foil) at the base of the tree.

12

To make a Candle Holder

We describe how to make a candelabrum for several tapers and a holder for a single candle.

Candelabrum

Materials:
- —Empty cardboard ribbon spool, about 3 inches in diameter by 1 inch high
- —Rice or sand
- —Scissors
- —Ribbon
- —Scotch tape
- —Half a dozen tapers
- —Regular foil

Instructions:
1. Tape up the hole on one side of the spool, and through the other hole fill the drum of the spool with rice or sand to make a solid base (fig. 1).
2. Cover the top and bottom of the spool with roughly cut-out circles of foil that are about 1 inch wider than the radius of the spool. With your fingers, mould the foil apron at top and bottom round the drum of the spool (figs. 2,3).
3. Cover the drum of the spool with a band of foil (as described in instructions 1 and 2, on pages 7-8). Join the ends with Scotch tape.

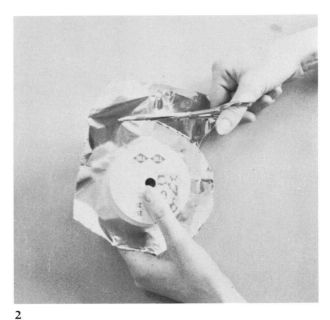

1

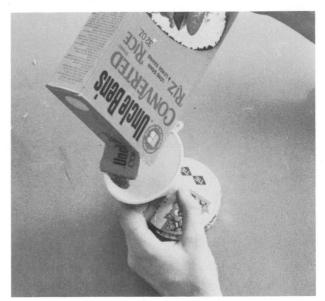

2

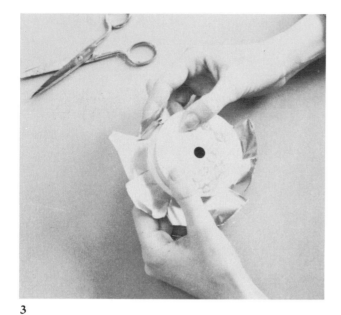

3

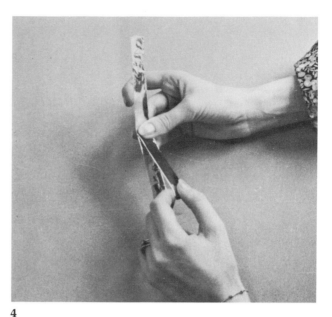

4

5

6

4. Make eight bands of foil, each about 12 inches long (see instructions 1 and 2 pages 7-8). Form each band into a double loop by doubling back the ends – a large loop by doubling back one end about two-thirds along the length of the band, and a small loop by doubling back the other end along the remaining third (figs. 4, 5). Crimp firmly the two ends at the point on the band at which they meet (fig. 6).

7

8

5. Open up the loops with your finger or a pencil, and tape the ends round the base of the spool, smaller loop uppermost.
6. If you wish, trim the top edge of the spool with coloured tinsel cord.
7. With pointed scissors, make small holes in the top of the spool. Push in the tapers and embed them firmly in the sand or rice (fig. 7). If you wish, you can put a small decoration on the top of the spool among the stems of the tapers.
8. Place the candelabrum on a cardboard circle covered with heavy-duty foil and trimmed with pieces of ribbon (fig. 8).

Candle Holder

Materials:
—Empty cardboard ribbon spool, about
  3 inches in diameter by 1 inch high
—Rice or sand
—Ribbon
—Scissors
—Scotch tape
—Candle
—Regular foil

Instructions:
1. Tape over the hole on one side of the spool, and through the other hole fill the drum of the spool with rice or sand to make a solid base.
2. Cover the top and bottom of the spool with roughly cut-out circles of foil that are about 1 inch wider than the radius of the spool. With your fingers, mould the foil apron at top and bottom round the drum of the spool.
3. Make twenty-four bands of foil, each about 4 inches long (as described in instructions 1 and 2, pages 7 8). Take two of these bands, loop them, and hold the four ends together to form a double loop. Crimp the four ends firmly together two or three times to join them.
4. Open up the loops with your finger or a pencil, and tape the ends to the top edge of the spool so that the double loop hangs over the side.
5. Surround the top of the spool with more double loops – eight in all.
6. Cover the drum of the spool with a strip of foil (edges folded in) that is the width of the drum. Tape the ends to hold in place.
7. Surround the base of the spool with eight single loops – each made from one 4-inch foil band (see instructions 3 and 4 above).
8. Glue a piece of ribbon around the drum.
9. Push the candle through the hole at the top of the spool and embed it firmly in the sand or rice.

To make a Christmas Angel

Materials:
- Sheet of heavy paper or light cardboard about 20 inches square
- Masking tape or staples
- Scissors
- Pins
- Rubber cement
- Blunt knitting needle
- Styrofoam ball about 2 inches in diameter
- Long skewer or pencil
- Scotch tape
- Tinsel cord
- Gift wrap or coloured paper
- Heavy-duty foil

design for angel's wings

1 square = 2"

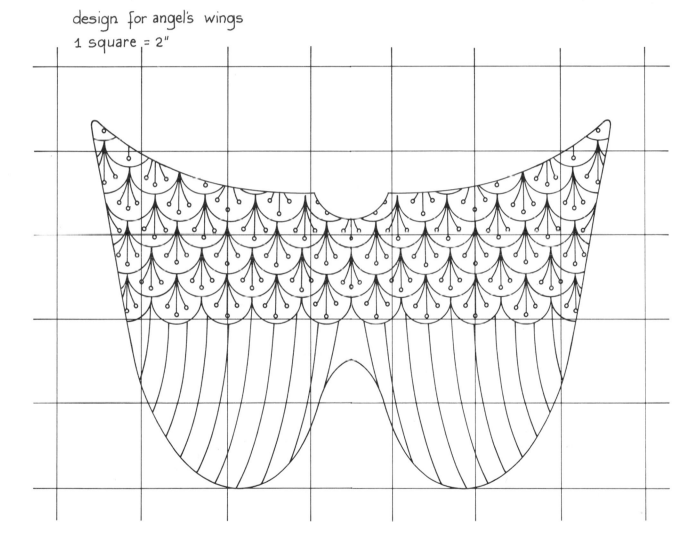

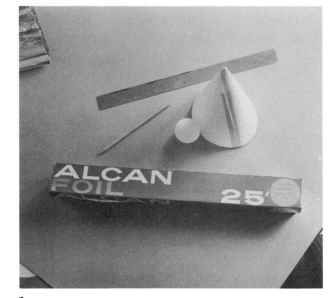

1

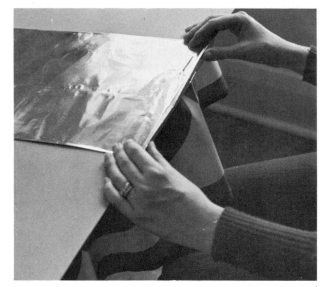

2

3

4

Instructions:

1. With the paper or cardboard, make a cone identical to that described in instructions 1, 2 and 3 for making the Christmas Tree (pages 25-7).

2. Tear off a 3-foot strip of heavy-duty foil. Fold in the foil about 4 inches on each side to reduce the width of the foil to 10 inches – or the same height as the cone (fig. 2).

3. Using the edge of a table, fold the 3-foot length of the foil into ½-inch pleats (fig. 3). Open up the pleats,

and form an open-ended cylinder by taping the pleated strip together along its 10-inch edges. Place the cylinder over the cone, and draw in the pleats at the top of the cone to form the body of the Angel (fig. 4).

4. To make the arms, tear off an 18-inch strip of foil, fold in about 4 inches on each side, and pleat, as with the body. Cut the strip in half across the pleats to give two pleated strips each 5 inches wide. Draw the pleats to-

5

6

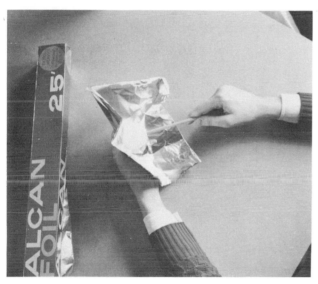

7

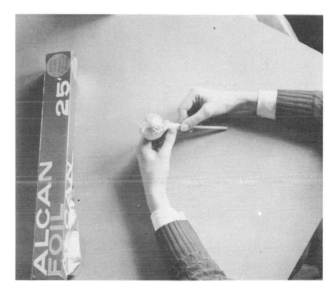

8

gether at the end of one of the strips, and tape this end at shoulder level to the pleats on one side of the body. Fan out the pleats at the other end. Repeat with the remaining 5-inch strip to form the other arm (figs. 5, 6).

5. To make the head, insert a skewer or pencil into the styrofoam ball. Cover the styrofoam ball with foil, leaving an overlap of foil that is lightly pressed round the pencil to serve as the neck (figs. 7, 8).

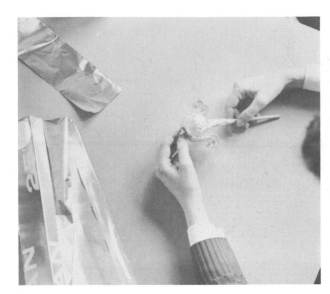

9

10

11

12

6. To make the curls, use two 8-inch bands of foil – see instructions 1 and 2 on page 7. With your fingers, curve each band into a suitable shape and attach to the top of the head with tape or pins (fig. 9).

7. To make the halo, tear off a 4-inch strip of foil and fold in each edge ½ inch along the 18-inch length. Then fold in half to form a band 1½ inches wide (fig. 10). Finally, make a small fold to join the open edges and form a reinforcement (fig. 11). With a pair of scissors cut out a leaf pattern along the edge with no reinforcement (see diagram); cut to within about ½ inch of the reinforcement (fig. 12). Shape into a circle, taking in tucks and taping where necessary (fig. 13). Attach to the back of the head with pins (fig. 14). To attach the head, push the skewer or pencil through the small hole at the top of the cone (fig. 15).

13

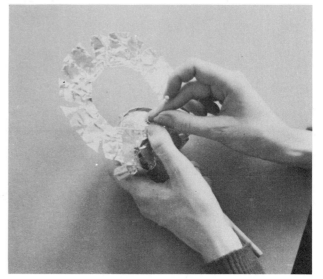

14

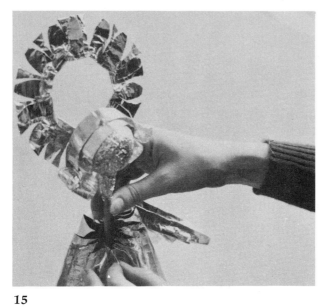

15

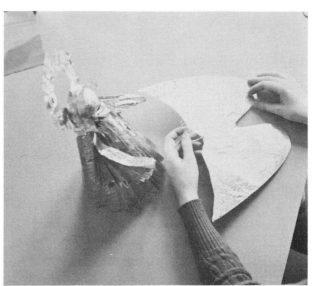

16

design for cutting the angel's halo

1 square = 1"

17

To make a Paper-Cup Angel

Materials:
   —Large paper cup
   —Scissors
   —Scotch tape
   —Pencil
   —Styrofoam ball about 1½ inches in diameter
   —Trim (tinsel cord, ribbon, medallions)
   —Regular foil
   —Heavy-duty foil
   —Gift wrap

8. At this stage, if necessary, lightly tape the body pleating at the top of the cone to prevent the pleating from opening out.

9. To make the wings, cut out the shape from heavy paper or light cardboard (see page 35). Use this shape to guide you in cutting out a piece of foil about 1 inch larger all round. With rubber cement, stick the foil to the paper or cardboard, folding the excess foil round the back. Then cut out another piece of foil the exact shape of the wings, and cement to the back. With a blunt needle or pencil, engrave a design on the foil covering of the wings (see diagram). Attach the wings to the back with tinsel cord running round the centre of the wings, round the neck, and tied with a bow at the front (figs. 16, 17).

10. To make the book, use gift wrap glued to one side of a folded rectangle of white paper. Tape to the pleated arms.

11. Place the finished Angel on a cardboard circle covered with foil.

Instructions:
1. Wrap the styrofoam ball in a piece of regular foil, moulding the overlap with your fingers to form a neck (fig. 2).

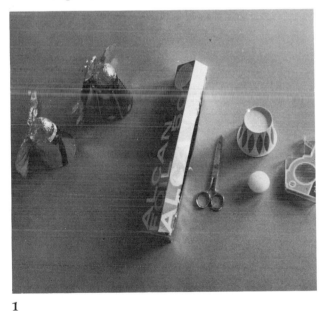

1

2

3

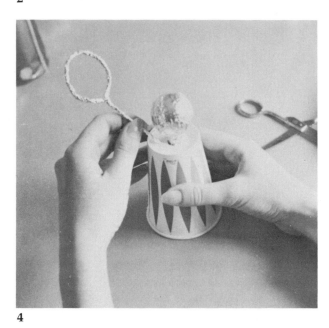

4

5

2. To make the halo, tear off a 2-inch strip of regular foil. Twist lengthwise and mould to form a fine "rope" (fig. 3). Leaving about 1 inch for insertion into the paper cup, form the rope into a circle.

3. Using scissors, punch two small holes in the top of the inverted cup, one in the centre and one at the edge. Force the neck of the foil-covered styrofoam ball into the central hole and the stem of the halo into the hole at the edge (fig. 4).

4. Wrap the paper cup in a sheet of gift wrap, tucking the overlap neatly inside the cup and securing with Scotch tape along the joins (figs. 5,6,7).

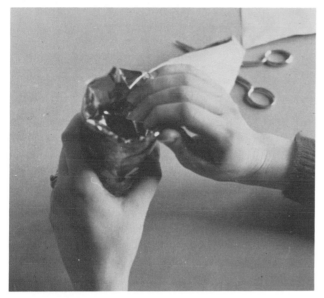

6
7

8

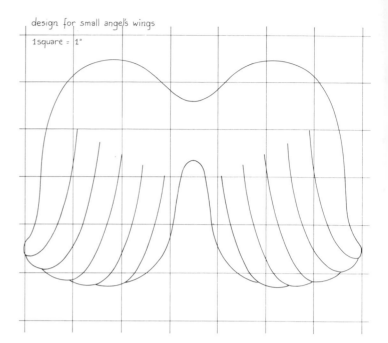

design for small angel's wings

1 square = 1"

9

5. Tear off a 5-inch strip of heavy-duty foil and, for added strength, fold in half to form a rectangle 9 inches by 5 inches. With a pencil, draw the wing shapes on the foil (see diagram) and cut out (fig. 8). Cut fringes at the base of the wings. Pinch together the central foil band joining the two wings, and tape to the back of the body (figs. 9,10).

6. Trim as desired with tinsel cord, ribbon or small medallions (fig. 11).

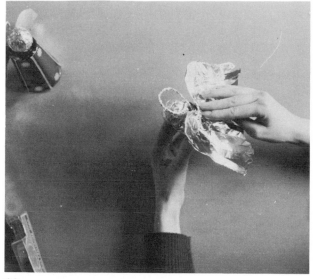

10

11

To make a Moon Decor

Astronaut

Materials:
- —Newspaper
- —Rubber cement or pins
- —Masking tape
- —Rickrack
- —Small cardboard box about 4½ inches by 2½ inches by 1½ inches
- —Heavy-duty foil

Instructions:
1. Separately make the rough shapes of the arms, legs, head and trunk of the astronaut out of pieces of newspaper. For example, to make the head, scrunch a double sheet into a ball and then wrap it in two single sheets (fig. 1).

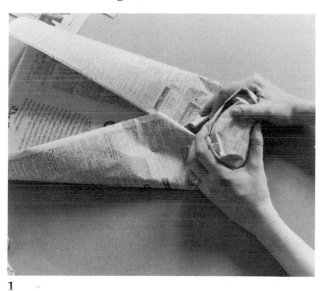

1

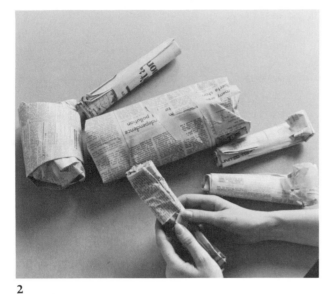

2

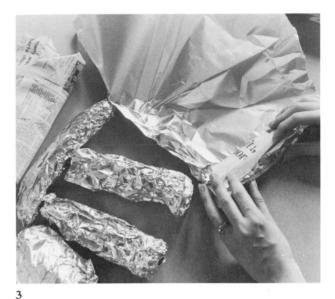

3

4

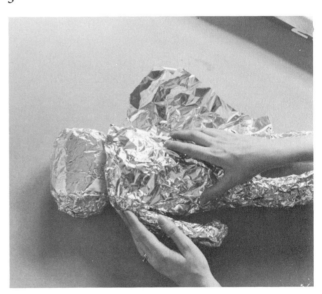

5

To make a leg, fold two double sheets the approximate length of the leg, roll up the paper to form the leg, and scrunch one end to form the foot (fig. 2). Hold the roughly shaped newspaper in place with masking tape. (Obviously the size of the finished astronaut depends on individual choice; the one depicted here is 18 inches high.)

2. Wrap each of the separate body parts in pieces of foil, moulding the foil with your fingers to achieve the desired shapes (fig. 3).

3. With masking tape, attach all the parts of the body together (fig. 4). Then cover the joins with further strips of foil, again moulding with your fingers to achieve the desired over-all shape (fig. 5).

4. Glue or pin the rickrack to the astronaut, following the design in the photograph on p. 47. Also draw a face on paper and glue to the front of the astronaut's head.

5. Cover a small cardboard box with foil, add an antenna made of foil rope (see instruction 5, page 66), and attach with masking tape to the astronaut's back.

6. If the astronaut's feet are sufficiently large, he will stand by himself. Otherwise, glue his feet to a circular disc cut from an aluminum pie plate or suspend him with thread attached to the ceiling with masking tape.

Rocket

Materials:
- Cardboard cylinder (from, say, a paper towel roll or foil box)
- Light cardboard, about 4 inches square
- Scissors
- Rubber cement
- Scotch tape
- Masking tape
- Acrylic paint and brush
- Regular foil

Instructions:
1. Glue foil strip to the cardboard and make a cone (fig. 1) with same diameter at the base as that of the cardboard cylinder (see instruction 3, page 27).

1

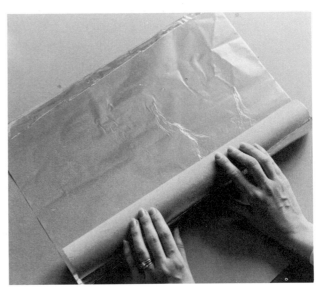

2

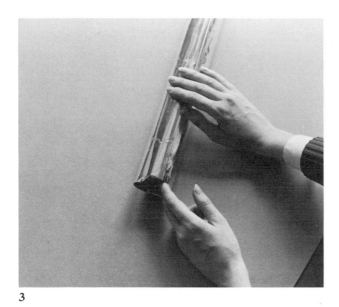

3

4

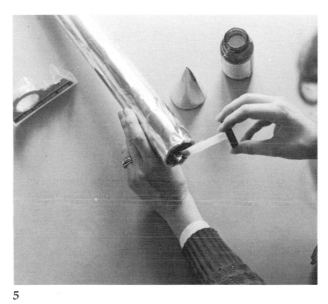

5

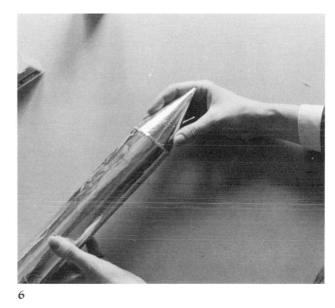

6

2. Wrap the cylinder in a sheet of regular foil, joining the edges with Scotch tape and folding in overlap at open ends of the cylinder (figs. 2,3,4). Bead one end with rubber cement and attach cone (figs. 5,6).

3. Using acrylic paint, colour a design on the rocket. For a birthday party, you might paint on the name of the birthday child.

4. Although the rocket will stand on its end, it is more effective to suspend it at an angle, with thread attached to a chandelier or the ceiling with masking tape.

5. To make the "tail" at the rear of the rocket, fringe a doubled-over 6-inch sheet of foil. Scotch tape the fringes to the rear of the rocket.

Background Setting

Materials:
—Small balloons
—Scissors
—Aluminum pie plates
—Small aluminum tart dishes
—Regular foil

Instructions:

1. Blow up the balloons. Then, for each balloon, tear off half a dozen 20-inch strips of foil and wrap them one at a time round the balloon. With each additional piece, cover the seams of the preceding pieces so that the foil is fairly evenly distributed. Flatten and mould the surface with your fingers as you add each piece, and be careful to leave a hole at the bottom so that the nozzle of the balloon is accessible. Deflate the balloon and remove it. The aluminum spheres so formed can be suspended with thread attached to the ceiling with masking tape; also, the holes can be widened by folding in the foil, and they can be used as containers (perhaps painted with children's names) for candies or favours.
2. To create a moon surface on the table, cut out the circular bases from several aluminum pie plates and tart dishes. Place the rims upside down on the table to form moon craters, and cover the table with sheets of foil, moulding the foil into the underlying craters.
3. Suspend satellite stars (see page 13) with thread attached to the ceiling with masking tape.

To make a Camelot Centrepiece

Knights

Materials:
—Styrofoam balls about 1½ inches in diameter
—Masking tape
—Rubber cement
—Pins
—Pink paper
—Gift wrap
—Regular foil

Instructions:

1. To make the head, tear off a 6-inch strip of foil and wrap it round a styrofoam ball (or tightly wadded ball of foil). Clench foil overlap in your fist to form neck and body.

2. To make arms and legs, tear off 2-inch strips of foil, and mould each strip with your fingers to form both limbs as one piece. Attach limbs to the body with masking tape or pins.

3. To make the armour, tear off a 4-inch strip of foil and wrap it round the body, ensuring that it hides any masking tape.

4. Draw a face on pink paper and pin at corners to styrofoam ball.

5. The sword of the horse rider is a toothpick covered with foil. The flag of the standard bearer is gift wrap doubled over and glued round a rope of foil. The knights may be pinned, glued, or taped to the castle (or the rider to the horse) to make them firm.

Castle

Materials:
- Aluminum pie plate
- Coffee tin about 6 inches in diameter
- Two sheets of light cardboard, 8 inches square and 25 inches by 2 inches
- Various sizes of cardboard boxes and cardboard cylinders
- Scissors
- Rubber cement
- Masking tape
- Scotch tape
- Gift wrap
- Regular foil

Instructions:
1. To make the base of the castle, wrap an inverted pie plate in gift wrap.
2. Tear off a 20-inch strip of foil and

wrap it round the tin. Tuck in the foil overlap at the open end, and secure the join with rubber cement or Scotch tape. Place the closed end of the tin on the base and secure with rubber cement. Decorate the foil surface with glued-on pieces of coloured paper and gift wrap.

3. Cut out a cardboard disc about 8 inches in diameter and cover both sides with foil. Bead the edge of the open end of the tin with rubber cement, and place the disc on top.

4. Glue foil on both sides of a strip of cardboard about 25 inches long and 2 inches wide. Serrate one of the longer edges. Join the two ends with masking tape, and attach to the cardboard disc with masking tape.

5. The towers and turrets are made from cardboard boxes and cylinders wrapped in foil or gift wrap. These are glued to the disc.

Horse

Materials:
- Scissors
- Gift wrap
- Silver rickrack
- Regular foil

Instructions:
1. Tear off an 18-inch piece of foil and make cuts in it as indicated in fig. 1. The segments resulting from the cuts form the head, body, legs, and tail of the horse. By twisting and pinching the foil with your fingers – modelling it as if it were clay – create the shape of the horse (figs. 2,3).
2. The mantle covering the horse is cut from gift wrap decorated with silver rickrack. The mantle is pinned to the back of the horse.

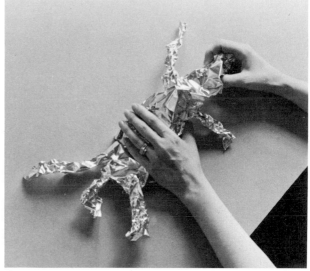

2

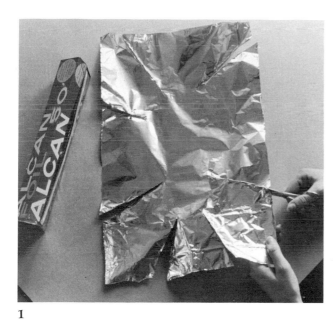

3

1

4

54

Dragon

Materials:
- —Scissors
- —Newspaper
- —Rubber cement
- —Pins
- —Gift wrap
- —Regular foil

Instructions:
1. Tear off a 36-inch sheet of foil and make cuts in it as indicated in fig. 1. As with the horse on the previous page, twist and model the foil to make the shape of the dragon, but this time incorporate a scrunched up piece of newspaper to pad out the belly (fig. 2).

1

2

2. Tear off another 36-inch sheet of foil, make similar cuts, and model it round the existing form of the dragon, shaping more precisely. To finish off neatly, wrap one or more 6-inch sheets of foil round the body and mould to the surface (fig. 3).

3. The fringe along the dragon's spine is cut from a strip of gift wrap that has been doubled over and glued. The fringe is pinned to the dragon's back.

4. The tongue, eyes and claws are cut from gift wrap and glued to the dragon.

Note: The technique of moulding foil with your fingers as if it were clay (as used in making the horse on page 53 and the dragon on page 54) is a very versatile one. By making suitable cuts in the foil, the kinds of objects that can be made in this way are limitless – animals, birds, ships, furniture, people, etc.

3

4

To make a Teen Age Party Setting

Food Dishes

Materials:
- —Plastic or china bowls
- —Scissors
- —Heavy-duty foil

Instructions:
1. Select a bowl, and tear off three sheets of foil large enough to cover the outside of the bowl with a 2-inch overlap all round (fig. 1).
2. Invert the bowl, and mould the first sheet (shiny side of foil down) over the bowl so that it takes up the shape (fig. 2). Flatten the overlap on the table.
3. Repeat with remaining two sheets (last sheet with shiny side of foil uppermost), moulding the foil into a cohesive structure. Remove the bowl.

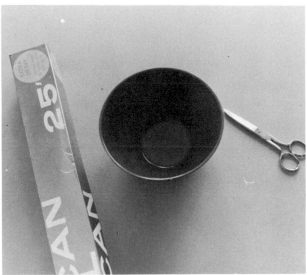

1

2

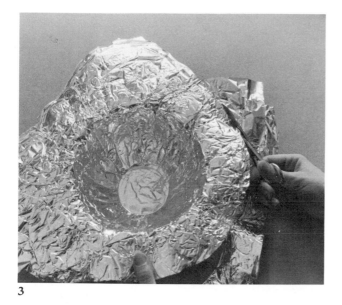

3

4

5

4. Cut a petal shape or points round the overlap (figs. 3,4).

Note: Using this technique you can make as many dishes as you wish, varying the shapes and sizes to meet your needs (fig. 5).

Flowers

Materials:
- Egg cup
- Scissors
- Wire or straws
- Masking tape
- Heavy-duty foil

Instructions:
1. Mould three strips of foil over inverted egg cup shape, as in instruction 1 on page 56. Cut petal shapes around the overlap or deeper into the flower. If you wish, put one flower inside another to make a double ring of petals.
2. Insert a foil-covered piece of wire or a foil-covered straw through the base of the flower and attach on the inside with masking tape.
3. Tear off a 4-inch strip of foil and fold in half lengthwise. Fringe along the open edges with scissors – cuts every 1/8 inch up to within about ¾ inch of folded edge. Roll up the fringed foil lengthwise, curling the fringes outwards. Tape into the centre of the flower, fringes uppermost.

Note: These foil flowers can be displayed either on their own or mixed among real flowers.

Braided Foil Numbers

Materials:
- Scissors
- Regular foil

Instructions:
1. Tear off three 45-inch sheets of foil and cut them in half lengthwise, to give six strips.
2. Working along each strip, scrunch the foil with your fingers and twist slightly so as to form a rope.
3. Clasping the ends of three ropes firmly, braid them together to form a flat pigtail. Finish off the ends by moulding them into the braid and cutting off any excess.
4. Keeping the braid flat, shape it into any number or letter desired. For our teen-age setting, we have made the number 16, requiring six ropes. The numbers can be laid flat on the table, propped up in the centre, or suspended from the ceiling.

3 Costume

Most of the costume pieces in this section are designed for children, for either their imaginative play or organised children's theatre. But adults will also find the techniques useful to make costumes for amateur dramatics or fancy-dress parties.

To make a Monarch's Crown

Materials:
—Light cardboard, 6 inches wide and about 24 inches long (as determined by the head size of the wearer)
—Pencil
—Pins
—Heavy cord
—Rubber cement
—India ink or black acrylic paint
—Fine steel wool
—Masking tape
—Styrofoam pieces
—Regular foil

Instructions:
1. With a pencil, draw a decorative pattern on the cardboard (see page 64).
2. Following the pattern, glue the heavy cord and styrofoam pieces (jewels) onto the cardboard. If

1

2

3

necessary, pin the cord and styrofoam in place until the cement is dry (fig. 1).

3. Tear off a 24-inch strip of foil, gently crinkle it, and then open it up again. Cover the front of the cardboard, including the relief design, with spray glue or a thin layer of rubber cement. Then place the crinkled foil carefully on the cardboard and, using your fingers, press it over the surface (fig. 2). Start at the centre and work outwards, being careful not to tear the foil when working over and around the relief design. A spoon may be helpful to smooth out the foil, but it is important not to obliterate the crinkled effect. Fold the excess around the back and glue to the back.

4. Working on areas about 6 inches square, blacken the foil surface with India ink (or acrylic paint), and rub off excess ink immediately with a rag or paper tissue. The crevices resulting from crinkling the foil should be left dark. If you wipe off too much ink, repeat with more ink. When you have completed the whole surface and the ink is dry, burnish the highlights of the relief with fine steel wool. (*Note:* This technique of crinkling the foil and then wiping it over with paint gives an attractive finish similar to forged metal. It is a technique that can be applied to other things you can make described in later sections.)

5. Join the two ends of the crown on the inside with masking tape.

6. Tear off eight strips of foil each 10 inches by 6 inches, and make them into bands 1½ inches wide (see instructions 1 and 2, pages 7-8). Loop the ends of each strip together and attach them with masking tape at intervals round the inside top edge of the crown.

Monarch's crown
1 square = 2"

To make a Mask

1

Materials:
- —Light cardboard about 12 inches by 4 inches
- —Scissors
- —Rubber cement or spray glue
- —String (or elastic)
- —Masking tape
- —Regular foil

Instructions:

1. Cut out mask shape from cardboard, including eye slits (fig. 1). Using the cardboard shape as a guide, cut out two pieces of foil – one the same size as the cardboard, the other roughly 1 inch bigger all round.

2. On the front of the cardboard shape, draw the underlying relief design with a pencil (see diagram). Glue along the line of the design, and then apply string to the glue to form a relief pattern – if necessary, you can use pins to hold the loops in place while the glue dries. To make the relief star in the centre of the mask, cut out the shapes from cardboard and glue in place (fig. 2).

3. Make a small hole on each side of the mask, and thread string (or elastic) through each hole from the back. Knot the ends.

4. Take the larger piece of foil, gently crinkle it, and then open it up again. Cover the front of the cardboard, including the relief design, with spray glue or a thin layer of rubber cement. Then place the crinkled foil carefully on the cardboard and, using your fingers, press it over the surface. Start at the centre and work outwards, being careful not to tear the foil when working over and

2

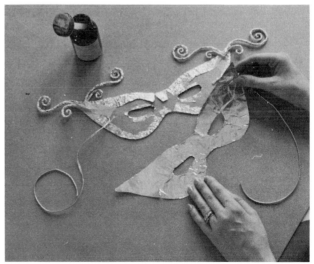

3

around the relief design (see instruction 3, page 62). Fold the excess around the back and glue to the back.

5. To make the two "whirligigs" at each corner of the mask, tear off four 2-inch strips of foil. Twist each strip lengthwise into a rope, mould firmly with your fingers, and bend to form the "whirligig" shapes. Attach to the corners of the mask at the back with masking tape.

6. Glue the other piece of foil, cut to the exact shape, to the back of the mask, with slits to accommodate string or elastic (fig. 3).

4

Note: If you prefer a lorgnette-type mask, you can attach a foil-covered stick with masking tape to one corner. In that case, you don't need the string (or elastic).

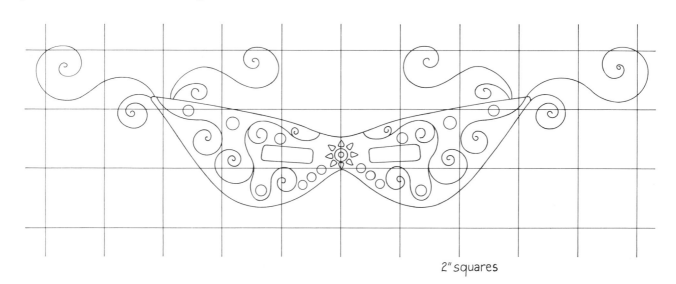

2" squares

68

To make a
Knight's Costume

Helmet

Materials:
   —Light cardboard about 26 inches by 10 inches
   —One round balloon
   —Masking tape
   —Rubber cement
   —Scissors
   —Heavy-duty foil

Instructions:
1. Cut out the light cardboard according to the shape in fig. 1. Join the ends with masking tape so that it fits the head of the wearer (fig. 2).
2. Blow up the balloon to fit tightly inside (fig. 3).
3. Tear off two 14-inch strips of foil. Mould them on top of one another over the balloon (fig. 4) as yet ignoring the cheek flaps. With your fingers, pinch and mould a crest from front to back on the top of the helmet (fig. 5). Tuck excess foil round the lower rim of the cardboard and nose guard (fig. 6).

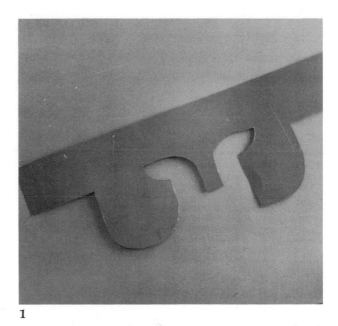

1

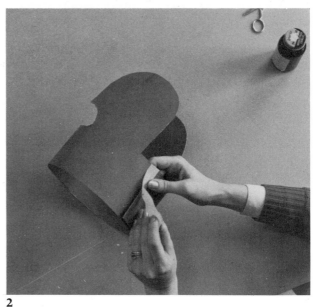

2

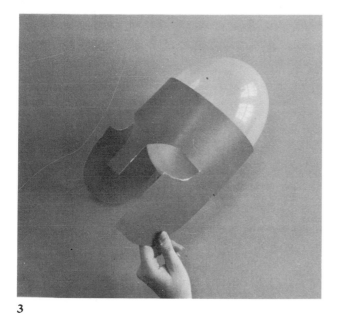

3

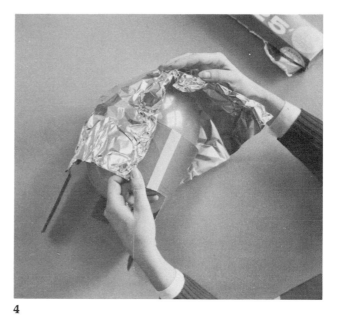

4

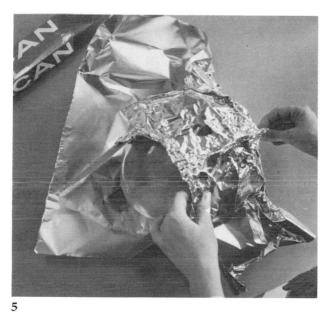

5

6

7

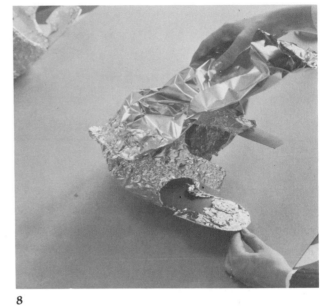

8

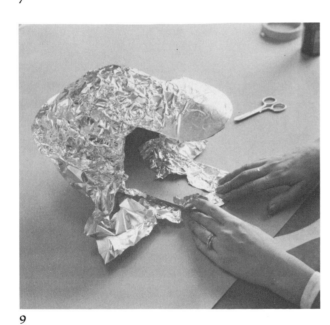

9

10

4. Remove the balloon.
5. Tear off one more 14-inch strip of foil. Glue the end of this strip to a cheek flap, trim and glue excess foil to back. Wrap over the head and glue the strip to the other cheek flap, moulding the foil to the shape of the helmet (including crest). Trim flap and glue excess foil to the back (figs. 7,8,9).

6. Secure with masking tape any loose
ends of foil inside the helmet and
firm up the structure with your
hands (fig. 10).

11

7. Make two ropes of foil, each about 6 inches long (see instruction 5, page 66). Bend into circles and glue one to each cheek flap (fig. 11).

Shield

Materials:
  —Stiff corrugated cardboard, about 18 inches by 24 inches
  —Razor knife
  —Scissors
  —Thick cardboard or styrofoam
  —String
  —Rubber cement
  —Spray glue
  —Heavy-duty foil

Instructions:
  1. Using a razor knife (or if you haven't got one, a pair of scissors) cut the stiff corrugated cardboard to the shape of the shield – about 23 inches high and 17 inches wide.
  2. Cut the pieces of the relief design (see diagram) from thick cardboard or styrofoam and glue to the front of the shield. Glue string to complete the relief.
  3. Punch two holes about 4 inches apart in the upper centre of the shield. Knot about three strands of string through these holes to form a handle; the knots should be at the front.
  4. Tear off a 24-inch sheet of foil and crinkle it (see instruction 3, page 62). Then spray glue the front of the shield, and carefully apply the foil. Glue overlap to the back of the shield.
  5. Tear off another 24-inch sheet of foil and cut to the exact shape of the shield. Spray glue the back of the shield and, after cutting a slot in the foil to fit over the string handle, apply it to the back.

Note: If desired, the front of the shield can be forged (see instruction 4, page 62).

design for knight's shield
1 square = 3"

Sword

Materials:
 —Stiff corrugated cardboard, about 36 inches long by 6 inches wide
 —Razor knife
 —Rubber cement
 —Spray glue
 —Scissors
 —String
 —Heavy-duty foil

Instructions:
 1. Using a razor knife (or pair of scissors) cut the stiff corrugated cardboard to the shape of the sword – about 36 inches long, with blade about 2 inches wide, and with the handle and guard each about 6 inches. Alternatively, you can make the sword from wood.
 2. Following the design (see diagram), glue string to one side of the sword. If you wish you may apply the design to both sides.
 3. Tear off a 30-inch sheet of foil. Cut off a 5-inch strip and, after spray gluing the blade, wrap the foil around. Fold round the point of the blade, and glue along the join.
 4. From the remaining piece of foil, cut out two pieces the shape of the handle – one the exact size and the other slightly larger. Assuming you have the relief design on only one side of the sword, crinkle the larger piece of foil, spray glue that side of the handle carrying the design, and apply the crinkled foil (see instruction 3, page 62). Glue overlap to the back. If desired, foil on this side of the handle can be forged (see instruction 4, page 62).
 5. Glue the remaining piece of foil (cut to the exact shape of the handle) to the back.

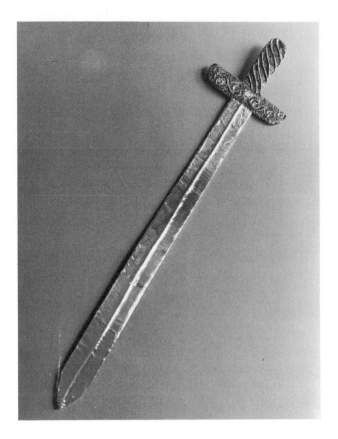

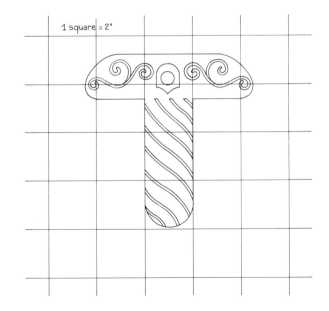

1 square = 2"

To make a Fairy Princess Costume

Wings

Materials:
- —2 wire coat hangers
- —Masking tape
- —Thin wire and pliers
- —Elastic
- —Regular foil

Instructions:
1. Bend the two coat hangers into wing shapes – see the diagram and fig. 1. Then cover the wire frames with 2-inch strips of foil (fig. 2).

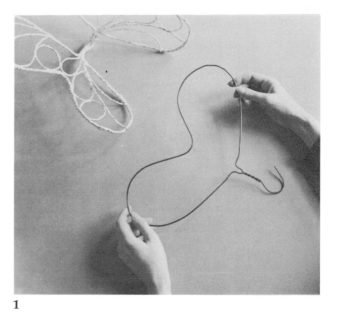

1

2

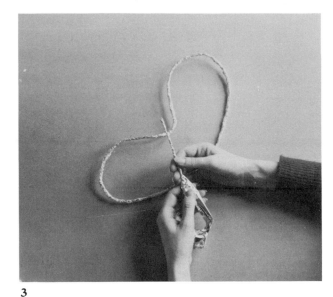

3

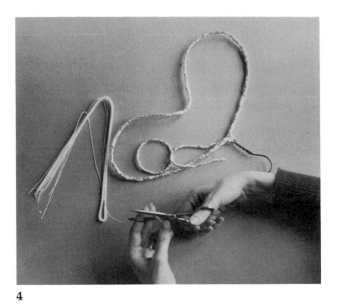

4

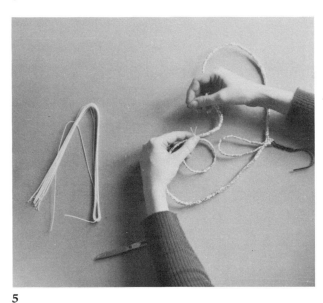

5

6

2. Tear off several 2-inch strips of foil, and twist and mould them with your fingers to form fine ropes (fig. 3). Following the diagram on page 77, bend the foil ropes into shape and attach them to each other and to the wing frames with thin wire (figs. 4,5).

3. Cut off the hooks on each hanger, leaving about a 3-inch length of wire on each. Using pliers, make a right-angled bend about halfway along each remaining 3-inch extension, overlap the two, and wind firmly with masking tape. Wrap a piece of foil around the join (fig. 6).

4. Attach two loops of elastic at the join, one to go round each shoulder.

design for ½ of fairy wings
1 square = 2"

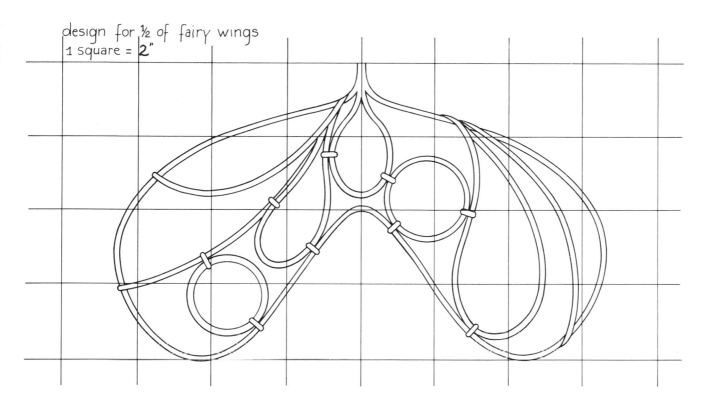

Crown

Materials:
—Thin wire and pliers
—Regular foil

Instructions:
1. Tear off a 24-inch piece of foil and form into a circular ring (see instructions 2 and 3, page 4). The diameter of the ring (approximately 6 inches) should be adjusted to fit the head that will wear it.
2. Tear off several 2-inch strips of foil, and twist and mould with your fingers to form fine "ropes". Following the pattern in the diagram, bend the foil ropes into shape and attach them to each other and to the head ring with thin wire; wire from garbage bag ties is very suitable.

Wand

Materials:
—Wooden stick about 20 inches long
—Cardboard
—Scissors
—Scotch tape
—Masking tape
—Rubber cement
—Regular foil

Instructions:
1. Wrap the stick in foil and tape along the join with Scotch tape.
2. Fold the cardboard and cut out two identical stars. Cut out two pieces of foil slightly larger than the cardboard stars, and glue to one side of each star. Glue overlap at the back.
3. With masking tape or rubber cement, attach the two stars parallel to each other at one end of the foil-covered stick.

1 square = 1"

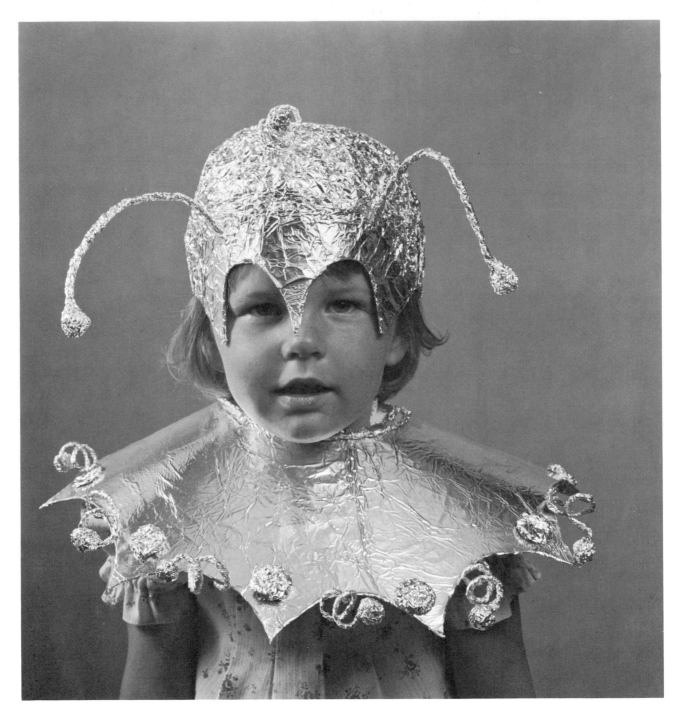

To make a Martian Costume

Helmet

Materials:
—Light cardboard, 4 inches wide and about 22 inches long (as determined by the head size of the wearer)
—One round balloon
—Masking tape
—Scissors
—Heavy-duty foil

Instructions:
1. Cut out semicircles from the cardboard so that it fits over eyes and ears.
2. With a 1-inch overlap, join the ends of the cardboard with masking tape.
3. Blow up the balloon to fit tightly inside the cardboard circle.
4. Tear off two 10-inch strips of foil. Mould them on top of one another over the balloon, working from side to side of the helmet and round the back. Tuck excess foil round the lower rim of the cardboard.
5. Tear off another 10-inch strip of foil, and this time working from front to back, mould the foil carefully over the projection between the eyes, over the head to the back of the helmet.
6. Deflate balloon and remove.
7. To make the antennae, tear off two 2-inch strips of foil, and twist and mould each of them into fine ropes with a bauble at one end. Punch a small hole above each eye circle, and insert the stems of the antennae through the holes. Secure them with masking tape on the inside of the helmet.
8. Make a "whirligig" in the same way as the antennae except spiral the stem. Punch a small hole through the centre of the helmet and secure stem with masking tape on the inside.

Collar

Materials:
—Light cardboard, at least 17 inches square
—Scissors
—Double-sided tape
—Masking tape
—Rubber cement
—Heavy-duty foil

Instructions:
1. From the cardboard, cut a disc with a diameter of about 17 inches (see instruction 1, page 25). Cut a hole with a diameter of about 5 inches (or larger, depending on neck size) in the middle of the disc. Scallop the outer edges of the disc, and cut a groove (tapering down to about 1 inch wide) from the outer edge of the disc to the hole in the middle (fig. 1).
2. Tear off an 18-inch square of foil. Glue to one side of the cardboard disc. Make cuts in the foil up to the edge of both the central hole and the points and curves of the scallop design, so that you can fold back the foil without tearing it. Glue the foil overlap to the back.
3. Make as many "whirligigs" as you have curves in your scalloped design – as described in instruction 7 for making the helmet. Attach the stems of the "whirligigs" with masking tape to the back of each scallop.
4. Make buttons (about ½ inch in diameter) by squeezing and moulding pieces of foil with your fingers. Glue a button to each point in the scalloped design.

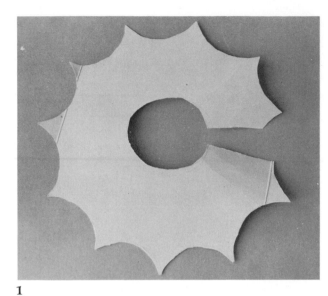

1

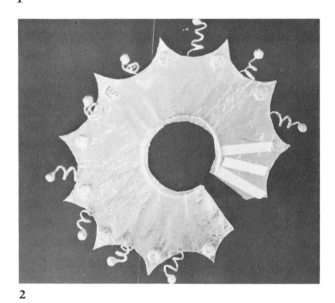

2

To make an Astronaut's Helmet

Materials:
—Large round balloon or inflatable beach ball
—Ribbon (foil or fabric)
—Scotch or double-sided tape
—Heavy-duty foil

Instructions:
1. Blow up the balloon to a diameter of at least 12 inches – more if you want the helmet to be larger.
2. Tear off seven pieces of foil, each about 40 inches long. Wrap the pieces one at a time around the balloon. With each additional piece, cover the seams of the preceding pieces so that the foil is fairly evenly distributed. Flatten and mould the surface with your fingers as you add each piece. And be careful to leave a hole at the bottom so that the nozzle of the balloon is accessible.
3. Deflate the balloon and remove it.
4. Turn in the edges round the hole where you removed the balloon, and create an oval-shaped hole about 8 inches by 6 inches.
5. Working through the oval hole, use both hands to mould and firm up the foil on the inside and outside of the helmet.
6. The oval hole allows the helmet to be fitted over the head – the longer diameter of the oval passes over the front and back of the head. The helmet is then turned through a right angle so that the longer diameter of the oval rests on the shoulders. Bearing this in mind, make a hole at the front and in the centre of the helmet. Cut and fold in

5. Glue a rope of foil about 17 inches long (as for the "whirligigs") around the outer edge of the central or neck hole.
6. Fit the collar round the neck and secure the overlap with double-sided tape – one piece of tape on the top side of the lower overlap and one piece on the bottom side of the upper overlap.

the foil to form a window about 7 inches wide and 5 inches high.

7. Trim the helmet window with foil or fabric ribbon. Use either double-sided tape or loops of Scotch tape to attach the ribbon. If the helmet is too loose on the head, a little padding inside the top and back will help it fit more firmly.

Note: If desired, a complete astronaut costume can be created by covering hockey gloves and rubber boots with foil. A foil-covered cardboard box with a foil-covered stick for the antenna makes a realistic back-pack.

4 Reliefs and Pictures

Using quite simple techniques and even without any special artistic talent, it is possible to create attractive reliefs, pictures, and sculptured figures for permanent display in the home. The reliefs and pictures may be framed or not, as you wish.

To make a Smiling Relief of the Sun

Materials:
—Piece of cardboard (or styrofoam) about 12 inches square
—White glue
—Acrylic paint
—Spray glue or rubber cement
—Heavy-duty foil

Instructions:
1. Draw design on cardboard sheet, using the diagram to guide you.
2. With a small nozzle top on the white glue, trace out the design. Ensure that the glue is thick enough to form a distinct ridge. Leave for at least half an hour to dry.
3. Cover the surface (including the design) with spray glue or a thin layer of rubber cement (fig. 1).

4. Tear off a 16-inch piece of foil, place carefully on the design, and, with a finger wrapped in a rag or paper tis-

1

2

sue, press foil over the surface. Start at the centre and work out towards the edges. A rubber on the end of a pencil is useful for pressing the foil into crevices.

5. Wrap the foil around the back of the cardboard, cutting a V-shape in each corner. Glue the foil to the back.
6. Use acrylic paint to colour the design.

2" squares

To make a Forged Relief of a Top-Hatted Man

Materials:
—Cardboard box, about 9 inches by 12 inches by 1 inch
—Rickrack
—Decorative stemmed buttons
—Safety pins
—Foil doilies
—India ink or black acrylic paint
—Pieces of heavy cardboard
—Rubber cement
—Decorative hook
—Regular foil

Instructions:
1. Cut out separately from the heavy cardboard the shapes that make up the man – hat, head, body, limbs, nose, eyes. Insofar as our design is taken from a five-year-old's drawing, we do not feel a diagram is necessary.
2. Following the design, glue the cardboard pieces to the top of the box, including the rickrack, safety pins and doilies. Punch holes for the button stems and also glue (fig. 1).
3. Cut out foil to the shape of the box so that there is overlap to fold round the back.
4. Gently crinkle the foil and, after covering the surface of the box with a thin layer of rubber cement, lay the foil over the relief, as described in instruction 3, page 62. Wrap the foil around the back of the box, cutting a V-shape in each corner, and glue the foil to the back.
5. Working on areas of approximately 6 inches square, blacken the surface with India ink (or acrylic paint), as described in instruction 4, page 62.
6. Attach the hook to the top of the box, and the relief is ready to hang.

Note: It is possible to make much larger and more elaborate reliefs with this technique, as shown in the following pages. Anyone with patience enough might consider creating a forged foil relief directly on a section of wall or even on a complete wall. Or, to lighten up a dark room, regular foil makes an attractive alternative to wallpaper, and may be applied to walls and ceilings with wallpaper paste.

Using a technique similar to that for the Top-Hatted Man (page 91), this forged foil relief was created out of heavy cardboard and cord at Ottawa's Canterbury High School, where Mr. John Topelko runs a flourishing art department. The relief is 48 inches by 42 inches and required several strips of foil to cover it.

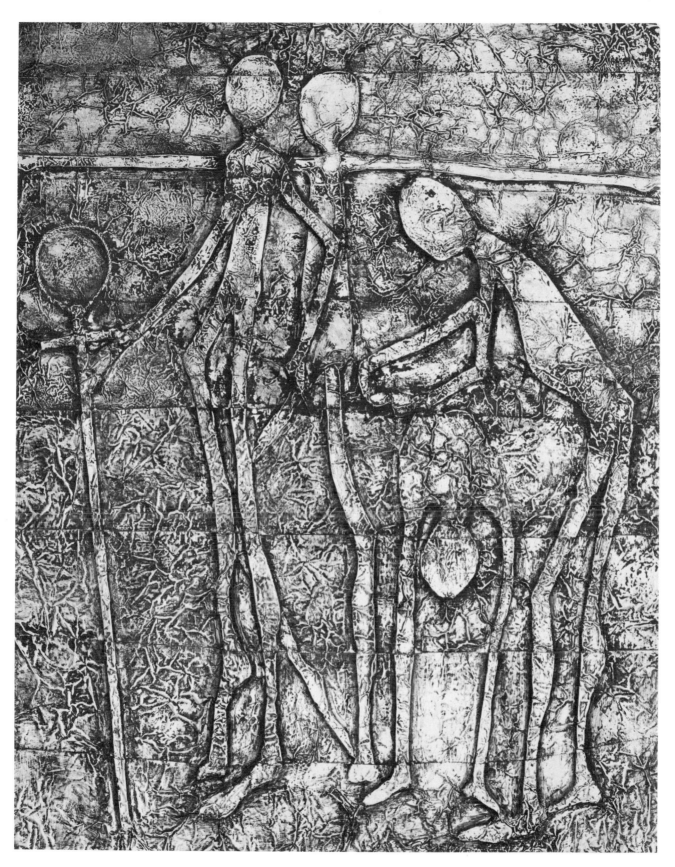

These forged foil reliefs were created by Mr. Giraudy's Grade 5 class at Northern Preparatory School in Toronto. Each is about 12 inches by 9 inches.

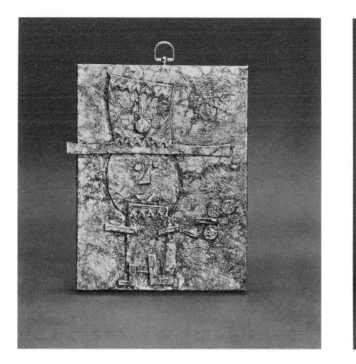

Jane Hinton's inspiration for this forged relief was the 1802 Murray Engine. The relief is 17 inches by 39 inches, and was first drawn, with ruler and compasses, on heavy cardboard and styrofoam, and then the shapes were cut out.

To make an Elegant Planter

1

2

Materials:
—Large plastic ice-cream container, about 7 inches in diameter and 5 inches high
—Heavy cardboard
—String
—Scissors
—Spray glue
—Rubber cement
—India ink (or black acrylic paint)
—Regular foil

Instructions:
1. Following the design (see diagram), glue the relief pattern of cardboard and string onto the plastic container (fig. 1).
2. Tear off a piece of foil slightly longer than the circumference of the container. Then crinkle the foil (see instruction 3, page 62) and, after spray gluing the outside wall of the container, apply the foil. Fold overlap round the top so that it comes about halfway down the container. Fold the rest of the overlap round the bottom edge and glue.
3. To produce the effect of forged metal, treat the relief surface with India ink or black acrylic paint (see instruction 4, page 62).
4. Cut a circle of foil the same size as the base of the container and glue to the bottom.

Note: This technique for making a planter can be applied equally well to making such things as a waste-paper basket or a lampshade.

design for planter
1 square = 2"

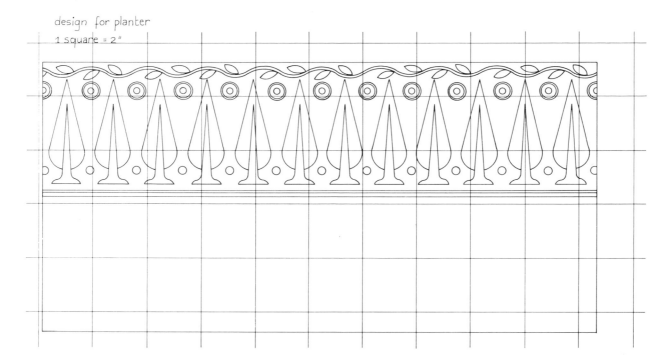

To make a Fancy Book Cover

Materials:
—Two sheets of light cardboard (Obviously, the dimensions of the cardboard will vary with the size of the book cover you want to make. In the cover depicted, the size is 8¾ inches wide and 11½ inches high.)
—Pieces of heavy cardboard
—String
—Rubber cement
—Scissors
—Spray glue
—India ink (or black acrylic paint)
—Two sheets of heavy coloured paper (or light cardboard)
—Regular foil

Instructions:
1. On the sheet of cardboard that will form the front of the book, glue on the string and cardboard design (see diagram).

2. Tear off a piece of foil slightly larger than the cardboard sheet and crinkle (see instruction 3, page 62). Spray glue the relief surface and apply the piece of foil. Glue overlap to the back.

3. Tear off another piece of foil, and repeat with the other piece of cardboard that will form the back of the book.

4. To produce the effect of forged metal, treat the foil surfaces on each cardboard sheet with India ink or black acrylic paint (see instruction 4, page 62).

5. On the inside of each cover, glue a sheet of heavy coloured paper (about ¼ inch smaller all round than the cover) to hide the ragged boundary of the foil overlap.

6. The cover shown here was bound with a plastic spiral. But there are several other methods – punching holes and binding with ribbon, using coloured tape along the spine, etc.

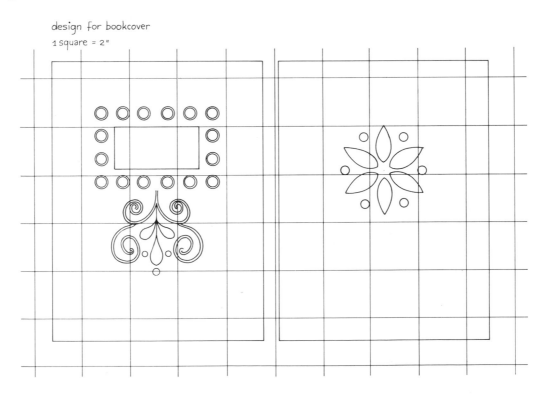

design for bookcover
1 square = 2"

To make a Decorative Box

Instructions:

Materials:
—Wooden chest-shaped box about 8½ inches long, 3½ inches wide and 5 inches high (as available from a hobby shop; any box, wood or cardboard, can be decorated in the way described)
—String
—Pieces of cardboard
—Small beads
—Styrofoam
—Spray glue
—Rubber cement
—Scissors
—India ink (or black acrylic paint)
—Two small hinges
—Regular foil

1. Following the design (see diagram), glue the string, pieces of cardboard, styrofoam and small beads onto the outside of the box to form the relief pattern (fig. 2).

2. The lid of the box and the box itself are covered with foil separately. To cover the lid, tear off two pieces of foil slightly larger than the lid ends. Crinkle the foil and, after spray gluing the ends, apply the foil (see instruction 3, page 62). Trim foil so that there is an overlap of about 1/8 inch – rather more under the lid. Glue overlap around the edge of the lid and also underneath.

3. Tear off a sheet of foil about 9 inches by 7 inches. Crinkle the foil and, after spray gluing the top, front and back

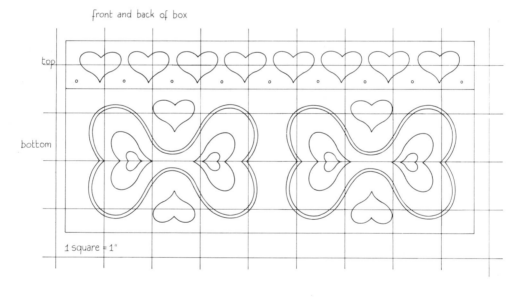

front and back of box

top

bottom

1 square = 1"

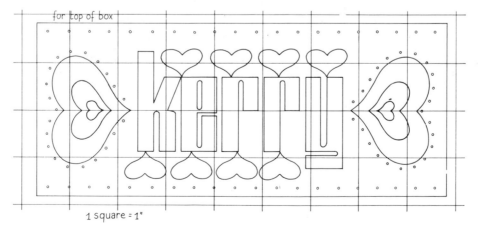

for top of box

1 square = 1"

1

2

of the lid, apply the foil, as in instruction 2 above. Trim excess foil to exact shape, except for the overlap to go under the lid. Glue overlap under the lid.

4. Repeat for the box, applying first two pieces of crinkled foil to the ends and then one piece of crinkled foil to the front, bottom and back.

5. To produce the effect of forged metal, treat the foil on both box and lid with India ink or black acrylic paint (see instruction 4, page 62).

6. Line the inside of the box and the lid with felt or hobby foil.

7. Attach the lid to the box with two small hinges.

3

design for side of box

1 square = 1"

top

bottom

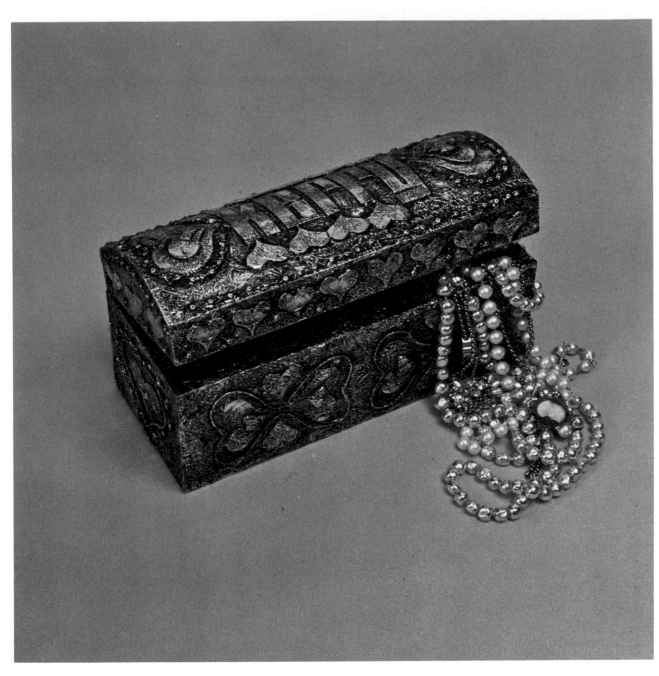

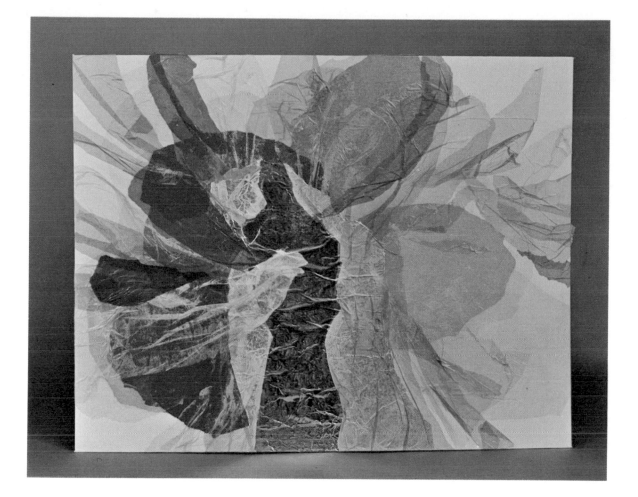

To make a Foil and Tissue Collage

Materials:
   —Canvas, canvas board, or cardboard
   —Acrylic polymer (matte medium and varnish, available from art supplies stores)
   —Coloured tissue and other materials
   —Regular foil

Instructions:
   1. The technique is simple. Cut or tear a piece of tissue or foil to the shape desired.
   2. Apply acrylic polymer on that area of the canvas where you wish to apply the tissue.
   3. Place the tissue on the polymer and then cover it with another layer of polymer.

Note: The collage shown here was done on a canvas board (24 inches by 30 inches) using coloured tissue and regular foil only. But interesting patterns can be achieved by incorporating other materials such as newspaper or gift wrap. You can either work to a preconceived design or create the design as you proceed. Tearing (rather than cutting) the foil or paper often gives rise to interesting shapes around which you can form a pattern. The pieces can be quite small (like ceramic tiles) or covering large areas up to 6 inches or more.

The Authors

Jane Hinton is a talented artist who won top honours while at St. Martin's School of Art in London, England. Her illustrations have appeared in leading British newspapers, her oils and mixed media works have been shown in Toronto and the United States, and her portraits hang in homes around the world.

Born in 1936 in Victoria, B.C., she attended high school in Toronto. She has lived in the United States, England, Montreal, and now lives in Toronto with her husband and sons.

Hugh Oliver has been involved with writing for most of his working life. He has edited numerous publications for Shell Petroleum and was publications manager for the Aluminum Company of Canada. He is currently editor of *Orbit*, O.I.S.E.'s journal for school teachers, has written a play widely produced on the continent and is also a successful writer of record lyrics.

Born in Epsom, England in 1929, he emigrated to Canada in 1966.